C# INTERVIEW QUESTIONS AND ANSWERS(EDITION:2021)

Vishal Garg

Copyrights

C# Interview Question and Answers

About the Book

C# interview questions is designed to help readers learn the concepts of C#.

This book covers all the concepts of C# with the help of Interview question and Answers.

More than 100 Questions are included in this book which are frequently asked in current scenario.

It covers all the key areas like generics , memory management , linq, Oop, design patterns etc.

Table of Contents

Q1. WHAT ARE TYPES IN C# ?

We have value types and reference types : -

Value Types	Reference Types
Default value : 0	Default value: Null
int, float, double, enums, structs etc.	Class, interface, delegates , string, arrays etc.

Q2. DIFFERENCE BETWEEN PARSE AND TRYPARSE ?

- To convert value from string to number format, we can either use Parse or tryparse
- Parse() method throws an exception if value cannot be parsed, whereas TryParse() returns bool value

Q3. WHAT ARE ARRAYS ?

An array is a collection of similar data types

Pros :-

- Arrays are strongly typed

Cons :-

- Arrays cannot grow in size once initialized - OutofRange exception if array size exceeds at run time.
- Depends on indexes to store or retrieve items – Index out of range exception, if pointed to wrong index number

Q4. WHAT IS DICTIONARY IN C# ?

1. A dictionary is a collection of (key ,value) pairs

2. **Keys** in dictionary must be **unique**
3. Dictionary provides fast lookup of values using keys
4. Namespace:- System.Collections.Generic

Q5. SPECIFY SOME USEFUL METHODS OF DICTIONARY ?

- **TryGetValue(key, out value)** :- this method will return bool type and outputs the value of key
- **Remove(key)** :- remove specific key from dictionary
- **Clear()**:- remove all items from dictionary

Q6. WHAT ARE LISTS ?

1. A list class is used to create a **collection of any type**
2. Unlike arrays, lists **size can grow dynamically**
3. Namespace:- System.Collections.Generic

Q7. WHAT IS THE USE OF ASYNC AND AWAIT KEYWORDS IN C# ?

- async and await keywords are used to create asynchronous methods.
- The async keyword specifies that a method is an asynchronous method and the await keyword specifies a suspension point.
- The await operator signals that the async method can't continue past that point until the awaited asynchronous process is complete. In the meantime, control returns to the caller of the async method.

Q8. WHAT ARE TYPE OF METHOD PARAMETERS?

1. Value parameter
2. Ref Parameter
3. Out Parameter
4. Params array parameter
5. Named parameter
6. Default Parameters or Optional Arguments

1. Value parameter : -

- Any changes made in the value type parameter it will not reflect the original data stored as argument
- By default we pass the parameter by value also known as value parameter

e.g.:-

```
using System;
public class Program
{
    public static void Main()
    {
        int i=0;
        Method(i);
        Console.WriteLine("Output: "+ i);
    }
    public static void Method(int j)
    {
        j = 100;
    }
}
//Output :-
Output: 0
```

2. Ref parameter:-

- To pass an argument with reference we need to use "**ref**" keyword.
- If any argument passed as reference then any **change** to the parameter in the called method is **reflected** in the calling method.
- Any **argument** being passed by reference **must be assigned** before passing it to the method. If it is not assigned then it will give compile time error. **Compilation error** : Use of unassigned local variable

e.g:-

```
using System;
public class Program
{
    public static void Main()
    {
        int i=0;
        Method(ref i);
        Console.WriteLine("Output: "+ i);
    }
    public static void Method(ref int j)
    {
        j = 100;
    }
}
//Output :-
Output: 100
```

3. *Out parameter:-*
- Used when you want to **return more than 1 value**
- To pass an argument we need to use "**out**" keyword.
- Any argument passed as out parameter **need not to be initialized**
- Out parameter **must be assigned inside the method** otherwise it will throw "variable not assigned" compilation error

e.g.

```
using System;
public class Program
{
    public static void Main()
    {
        int i=0;
        Method(out i);
        Console.WriteLine("Output: "+ i);
    }
```

```
   public static void Method(out int j)
   {
      j = 100;
   }
}
//Output :-
Output: 100
```

4. *Params type:-*
1. The **'params'** keyword is used with a method parameter.
2. The parameter used with 'params' should be a **single dimensional array** otherwise compilation error will be thrown
3. You can send comma separated values or an array or no arguments
4. Any number of arguments can be passed
5. All arguments I.e. params array should be of **same type**
6. One method should have only 1 params array, **2 params array are not allowed in method** otherwise compilation error will be thrown.
7. 'params' array **must be last parameter** in a method otherwise compilation error will be thrown

e.g.

```
public static void ParamsType()
   {
      int[] i = { 1 };
      someMethodParams(10, i);
      Console.WriteLine("value : " + i[0]);
      Console.ReadLine();
   }

   private static void someMethodParams(int j, params int[] i)
   {
      i[0] = 100;
      j = 100;
   }
```

```
//output
value : 100
```

5. Named parameter

- Using this feature we can specify the **value of a parameter by parameter name** regardless of its ordering in method.
- All the named parameters must appear after fixed arguments otherwise following error will be thrown.

Compilation error : Named argument specifications must appear after all fixed arguments have been specified.

Advantages of Named Parameter

- Named parameter provide us the facility to do not remember the parameter ordering.
- Improves the readability of code.
- Easy to understand.
- Due to readability it also reduces the chances of bug in application.

Disadvantages of Named Parameter

- Its performance is slower as compared to fixed argument. It should be avoided if it does not change the readability and understanding of code to a great extent.
- Due to slower performance we can also say that it is syntactic sugar over fixed parameter calls.

e.g.

```
using System;

public class Program
{
    public static void Main()
    {
        int x,y,z;
        Method(y:20, x:10, z:30);


    }
```

```
    public static void Method(int x,int y ,int z)
    {
        Console.WriteLine("x : "+ x);
        Console.WriteLine("y : "+ y);
        Console.WriteLine("z : "+ z);
    }
}
//Output :
x : 10
y : 20
z : 30
```

6. Default Parameters or Optional Arguments

- Any call can omit arguments for optional parameter but it must specify the value for required (fixed) parameter.
- Optional parameter must be defined after any required parameter.
- While calling the method having optional parameter if we provide value for an optional parameter then we must provide value for all preceding optional parameters.

e.g.

```
public static void DefaultType()
    {
        int x, y, z;
        someMethodDefault(10,5);
    }

    private static void someMethodDefault(int x, int y = 1,int z =2)
    {
        Console.WriteLine("x : " + x);
        Console.WriteLine("y : " + y);
        Console.WriteLine("z : " + z);
        Console.ReadLine();
    }
//output :
```

```
x : 10
y: 5
z: 2
```

Q9. What is Difference between out and ref ?

Out	ref
Argument passed need not be initialized	Argument passed must be initialized otherwise compilation error
Argument must be assigned inside calling method otherwise compilation error will be thrown	Argument need not be initialized inside calling method

Q10. What is a class ?

- A class is a template which is used to create complex custom types
- Consists of data (fields) and behavior (methods)

Q11. What is a Constructor?

1. Purpose of constructor is to initialize class fields
2. Constructor is automatically called when an instance of class is created
3. Do not have return types
4. Have Same name as class
5. A default parameter-less constructor is always called, if no constructor is provided
6. Constructors can be overloaded by number and type of parameters

Q12. What is a Static Constructor?

1. Static Constructor is used to initialize static fields of a class
2. Called only once
3. Called before instance Constructors

4. Do not have access modifiers otherwise will throw compile error "access modifiers are not allowed"
5. They are parameter less otherwise will throw compile error "a static constructor must be parameterless"
6. Only one static constructor is allowed

Q13. WHAT ARE PILLARS OF OOP?

1. Inheritance
2. Encapsulation
3. Abstraction
4. Polymorphism

Q14. WHAT'S PURPOSE OF INHERITANCE?

1. Code reusability
2. Reduce time and errors

Q15. WHAT ARE FEATURES OF INHERITANCE?

Syntax: -

```
Public class DerivedClass : BaseClass
{
// implementation
}
```

1. C# supports only single class inheritance
2. C# supports multiple interface inheritance
3. Base classes are automatically instantiated before derived class
4. Parent class constructor executes before child class constructor
5. Child class is specialization of base class

Q16. EXPLAIN VIRTUAL, OVERRIDE AND NEW KEYWORDS ?

Virtual :-

The virtual keyword is used to modify a method, property, indexer, or event declared in the base class and allow it to be overridden in the derived class.

Override :-

The override keyword is used to extend or modify a virtual/abstract method, property, indexer, or event of base class into derived class.

New :-

The new keyword is used to hide a method, property, indexer, or event of base class into derived class.

Q17. WHAT IS DATA / METHOD HIDING?

- **Hides** the methods or fields data of the base class from derived class
- Using '**new**' keyword, we can hide base method implementation from derived class
- Also known as Method Shadowing

```
// METHOD HIDING - new operator will hide base class method
using System;

public class A
{
    internal string name= "A Field";
    public void Print()
    {
        Console.WriteLine("A Method," + name);
    }
}
public class B : A
{
    new string name = "B Field";
    new public void Print()
    {
        Console.WriteLine("B Method," + name);
    }
```

```
}
public class Program
{
    public static void Main()
    {
        B obj = new B();
        obj.Print();
        A obj1 = new B();
        obj1.Print();
    }
}
//Output: -
//B Method,B Field
//A Method,A Field
```

Note: -

- Base class can hold the reference of child class but child class cannot hold the reference of base class.

Q18. WHAT IS POLYMORPHISM ?

Polymorphism provides the ability to a class to have multiple implementations with the same name

1. Invoking derived class methods through a base class reference during runtime
2. In base class method is declared **virtual** while in derived class it is declared as **override**
3. **Virtual** keyword states that **method can be overridden in derived class**
4. We **cannot override method without** declaring it as **virtual in base class** otherwise it will throw compile time error

e.g.

// METHOD Override - virtual/override operator will override base class method

```csharp
using System;

public class A
{
    internal string name= "A Field";
    virtual public void Print()
    {
        Console.WriteLine("A Method," + name);
    }
}
public class B : A
{
    string name = "B Field";
    override public void Print()
    {
        Console.WriteLine("B Method," + name);
    }
}
public class Program
{
    public static void Main()
    {
        B obj = new B();
        obj.Print();
        A obj1 = new B();
        obj1.Print();
    }
}
//Output :-
//B Method,B Field
//B Method,B Field
```

Q19. WHAT ARE TYPES OF POLYMORPHISM ?

There are two types of polymorphism in C#:

- Static / Compile Time Polymorphism.
- Dynamic / Runtime Polymorphism.

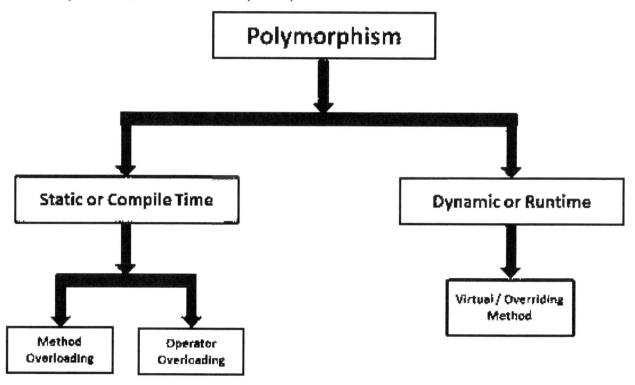

Static or Compile Time Polymorphism

1. It is also known as Early Binding.
2. Method overloading is an example of Static Polymorphism.
3. In overloading, the method / function has a same name but different signatures.
4. It is also known as Compile Time Polymorphism because the decision of which method is to be called is made at compile time.
5. Overloading is the concept in which method names are the same with a different set of parameters.

Dynamic / Runtime Polymorphism

1. Dynamic / runtime polymorphism is also known as late binding.

2. Here, the method name and the method signature (number of parameters and parameter type must be the same and may have a different implementation).
3. Method overriding is an example of dynamic polymorphism.
4. Method overriding can be done using inheritance.
5. With method overriding it is possible for the base class and derived class to have the same method name and same parameters.
6. The compiler will decide which method to call at runtime and if no method is found then it throws an error.

Q20. DIFFERENCE BETWEEN STATIC AND DYNAMIC POLYMOPHISM ?

Static or Compile Time Polymorphism	Dynamic / Runtime Polymorphism
Early binding	Late binding
Method overloading	Method overriding
Method has same name but different signatures	Method has same name and same parameters
Resolved at compile time	Resolved at run time

Q21. DIFFERENCE BETWEEN METHOD HIDING AND METHOD OVERRIDING ?

METHOD OVERRIDING	METHOD HIDING
In method overriding, you need to define the method of a parent class as a virtual method using **virtual** keyword and the method of child class as an overridden method using override keyword.	In method hiding, you just simply create a method in a parent class and in child class you need to define that method using **new** keyword.
In method overriding, when base class reference variable pointing to the object of the derived class, then it will call the overridden	In the method hiding, when base class reference variable pointing to the object of the derived class, then it will call the hidden

method in the derived class.	method in the base class.

Q22. WHAT IS METHOD OVERLOADING ?

1. Multiple methods with same name but different signatures
2. Functions can be overloaded based on the :-
   - Number (number of arguments passed)
   - Type (int, string, float etc.)
   - Kind (value, ref, out etc.)

   Of parameters.
3. Return type is not a criteria for overloading

Q23. WHAT IS ENCAPSULATION AND HOW IT IS IMPLEMENTED ?

- Encapsulation is the procedure of encapsulating data and functions into a single unit (called class).
- The need of encapsulation is to protect or prevent the code (data) from data corruption.
- Instead of defining the data in the form of public, we can declare those fields as private.

Encapsulation can be implemented in 2 ways to access Private data members: -

- Accessors (Getter method) and mutators (Setter method)
- Properties

Q24. WHAT ARE PROPERTIES?

We use get and set accessors to implement properties

1. **Read/Write property**: - Property with both get and set accessor
2. **Read only property** :- Property with get accessor only
3. **Write only property**: - Property with set accessor only

4. **Auto-implemented property**: - If there is no logic in property accessor, then we can use this property. Also, compiler creates a private anonymous field that can be accessed using get and set accessor of property.

Q25. WHAT IS ABSTRACTION AND HOW TO ACHIEVE IT?

- It is used to display only necessary and essential features of an object to outside world
- Hiding can be achieved using **'Private'** access modifiers.

we can achieve abstraction in 2 ways - by using:-

1. Abstract classes
2. Interface

Q26. WHAT IS AN INTERFACE?

1. Just like class, Interfaces contains properties, methods, delegates etc. But **only declarations and no implementations**
2. **'Interface'** keyword is used to create interfaces
3. **No Implementation** :- Implementation of any interface member cannot be provided otherwise complier error
4. **Public By default** :- Interface members are public by default otherwise will throw compile time error
5. **Fields not allowed** :- Interfaces cannot contain fields otherwise will throw compile time error
6. A class implementing interface must implement all the members of interface otherwise will throw compile time error.
7. A class can inherit more than 1 interfaces
8. If a class is implementing both interface and class at same time, then a class must be implemented first otherwise compile error will be thrown

Public class DerivedClass : BaseClass , IInterface	✅
Public class DerivedClass : IInterface , BaseClass	✖

9. Interfaces can inherit another interface

10. Instance of interface cannot be created but interface reference variable can point to derived class object.

e.g.

```
using System;
interface IInterface
{
  void Print();
}
public class ClassA
{
  public void printA()
  {
    Console.WriteLine("printA");
  }
}
public class ClassB : IInterface
{
  public void printB()
  {
    Console.WriteLine("printB");
  }
  public void Print()
  {
    Console.WriteLine("print from Interface");
  }
}

public class Program
{
  public static void Main()
  {
    IInterface obj = new IInterface(); // error
    IInterface obj = new ClassA(); //error
   //Object reference variable pointing to derived class: -
```

```
        IInterface obj = new ClassB();
    //Object reference variable can access members of parent
interface only        and not members of derived class
        obj.Print();
        obj.PrintB(); //error
        ClassB objB = new ClassB();
        objB.printB();
    }
}
```

Q27. WHAT IS AN EXPLICIT INTERFACE ?

A class inherits two interfaces and both have same method names. How should the class implement both interfaces?

- By using Explicit Interface, we can solve this problem
- Access modifiers are not allowed on explicit interface members.
- Explicit interface members cannot be called using class objects but only through interface reference variable

e.g.

```
using System;

interface IInterfaceA
{
    void Print();
}

interface IInterfaceB
{
    void Print();
}

public class ClassA : IInterfaceA, IInterfaceB
{
```

```
// ACCESS MODIFIERS NOT ALLOWED
  void IInterfaceA.Print()
  {
    Console.WriteLine("print from Interface A");
  }

  void IInterfaceB.Print()
  {
    Console.WriteLine("print from Interface B");
  }
}

public class Program
{
  public static void Main()
  {
    ClassA obj = new ClassA();
//ONLY BY USING INTERFACE VARIABLES, WE CAN ACCESS EXPLICIT
//INTERFACE MEMBERS
    ((IInterfaceA)obj).Print();
    ((IInterfaceB)obj).Print();
  }
}
//OUTPUT :-
//print from Interface A
//print from Interface B
```

Q28. WHAT ARE ABSTRACT CLASSES?

1. An abstract class is an **incomplete class** or special class that can't be instantiated.
2. The purpose of an abstract class is to provide a **blueprint for derived classes**
3. We can only use an **abstract class as a base class** and all derived classes must implement abstract definitions.

4. Using **'override'** keyword an abstract method must be implemented in all non-abstract classes
5. **No instantiation** :- we cannot instantiate a Abstract class.
6. **'abstract' keyword** is used before class to mark it as abstract class.
7. An abstract class may contain abstract methods or properties but not mandatory. It can contain both abstract and non-abstract methods, properties etc.

Abstract Class Features

An abstract class can : -

1. inherit from a class and one or more interfaces.
2. implement code with non-Abstract methods.
3. **Have modifiers** for methods, properties etc.
4. **Have constants and fields**.
5. **implement a property**.
6. **Have constructors or destructors**.
7. not be inherited from by structures.
8. **not support multiple inheritance**.
9. **Not be sealed**
10. If a derived class do not wish to provide implementation of base abstract class than derived class should be marked as abstract class

Abstract methods

Abstract methods cannot have a body. They need to be implemented in derived classes.

e.g.

```
using System;

public abstract class ClassA
{
   public void Print()
   {
     Console.WriteLine("classA print");
```

```
    }
    abstract public void Show();

}
public class ClassB : ClassA
{
    override public void Show()
    {
        Console.WriteLine("classA show");
    }
}

public class Program
{
    public static void Main()
    {
        ClassB obj = new ClassB();
        obj.Print();
        //USING BASE CLASS REFERENCE VARIABLE
        ClassA objA = new ClassB();
        objA.Show();
    }
}
//OUTPUT :
//classA print
//classA show
```

Q29. DIFFERENCE BETWEEN ABSTRACT CLASSES AND INTERFACE?

Abstract Class	Interface
Can have Implementation for some of its non-abstract members.	Cannot have implementation for any of its members.
Can have Fields	Cannot have Fields
Can have access modifiers	Cannot have access modifiers

DELEGATES

Q30. WHAT ARE DELEGATES ?

- A Delegate is a **type-safe functional pointer**
- Signature of Delegate **should match signature of Function**, that is why delegates are type safe functional pointers
- A Delegate will **point to a function** and when we call a delegate, the function will be invoked
- A delegate is similar to Class I.e., you can create instance of it and you will pass the function name as a parameter in delegate constructor and it is to this function that the delegate will point to.
- Delegate makes our code **reusable**
- We can **pass functions as parameter** in other function using delegate

Syntax : <access specifier> **delegate** <Method syntax>

Step1 : Define a delegate

e.g. Public **delegate** void FunctionDelegate(arg1, arg2...);

Step2 : Next, we need to create instance of delegate just like class objects

e.g. FunctionDelegate del = new FunctionDelegate(name of method);

del(arguments);

e.g.1 :

```
using System;
public delegate void delegatePrint();

public class Program
{
    public static void Main()
    {
        delegatePrint del = new delegatePrint(print1);
        del();
    }
```

```
        public static void print1()
        {
                Console.WriteLine("Print 1");
        }
}


//Output :
// Print 1
```

e.g. 2 :

```
using System;
using System.Collections.Generic;

public delegate bool delPromoted(Employee emp);

public class Program
{
        public static void Main()
        {
                List<Employee> empList = new List<Employee>();
                empList.Add(new Employee()
                {Id = 1, Name = "John", Salary = 1000, Experince = 1});
                empList.Add(new Employee()
                {Id = 2, Name = "Mike", Salary = 5000, Experince = 5});
                empList.Add(new Employee()
                {Id = 3, Name = "Rita", Salary = 3000, Experince = 2});
                empList.Add(new Employee()
                {Id = 4, Name = "Bob", Salary = 8000, Experince = 6});

                delPromoted delObj = new delPromoted(IsPromoted);
                Employee.PromoteEmployees(empList,delObj);
        }
```

```csharp
        public static bool IsPromoted(Employee emp)
        {
                if (emp.Experince >= 2)
                {
                        return true;
                }
                else
                        return false;
        }
}

public class Employee
{
        public int Id
        {
                get;
                set;
        }

        public string Name
        {
                get;
                set;
        }

        public int Salary
        {
                get;
                set;
        }

        public int Experince
        {
                get;
                set;
```

```
            }

public static void PromoteEmployees(List<Employee>
empList,delPromoted delObj)
        {
                foreach (var item in empList)
                {
                        if (delObj(item))
                        {
                                Console.WriteLine(item.Name + " promoted");
                        }
                }
        }
}
```

e.g.3 : Same can be achieved by using lambda expression :-

```
using System;
using System.Collections.Generic;

public delegate bool delPromoted(Employee emp);

public class Program
{
        public static void Main()
        {
                List<Employee> empList = new List<Employee>();
                empList.Add(new Employee()
                {Id = 1, Name = "John", Salary = 1000, Experince = 1});
                empList.Add(new Employee()
                {Id = 2, Name = "Mike", Salary = 5000, Experince = 5});
                empList.Add(new Employee()
                {Id = 3, Name = "Rita", Salary = 3000, Experince = 2});
                empList.Add(new Employee()
                {Id = 4, Name = "Bob", Salary = 8000, Experince = 6});
```

```csharp
        // Delegate using Lambda expression

        Employee.PromoteEmployees(empList,emp=>emp.Experince>=2);
        }


}

public class Employee
{
        public int Id
        {
                get;
                set;
        }

        public string Name
        {
                get;
                set;
        }

        public int Salary
        {
                get;
                set;
        }

        public int Experince
        {
                get;
                set;
        }

public static void PromoteEmployees(List<Employee>
empList,delPromoted delObj)
```

```
        {
                foreach (var item in empList)
                {
                        if (delObj(item))
                        {
                                Console.WriteLine(item.Name + " promoted");
                        }
                }
        }
}
```

Q31. WHAT ARE MULTICAST DELEGATES?

- Multicast Delegate is a delegate which has **reference to more than one function.**
- When Multicast Delegate is invoked, **all the functions** a delegate is pointing to **gets invoked**
- Multicast Delegate **invokes the method in same order** in which they are added
- If a multicast delegate has a return type then only the value of last invoked method will be considered.

There are 2 approaches to create multicast delegates:-

- **+ or +=** :- To **register** a method with delegate
- **- or -=** :- To **de-register** a method with delegate

e.g.

```
using System;

public delegate void delegatePrint();
public class Program
{
        public static void Main()
        {
```

```
// del is a multicast delegate, since it is pointing to multiple methods
// methods are called in the same order in which they are referenced
            delegatePrint del = new delegatePrint(print1);
            del += print2;
            del += print3;
            del -= print2;
            del();
    }
    public static void print1()
    {
            Console.WriteLine("Print 1");
    }
    public static void print2()
    {
            Console.WriteLine("Print 2");
    }
    public static void print3()
    {
            Console.WriteLine("Print 3");
    }
}

//Output :
// Print 1
//Print 3
```

Q32. WHERE TO USE MULTICAST DELEGATES ?

Multicast delegate makes implementation of **observer pattern** very simple.
Observer pattern is also called as **publish/subscribe pattern**.

Q33. WHAT IS FUNC DELEGATE IN C# ?

Func<T,TResult> is a generic delegate included in the System namespace.

1. It has **zero or more input parameters** and **one out parameter**.
2. The **last parameter** is considered as an **out parameter**.
3. 17 overloaded variations in Func i.e. we can pass atleast 16 input parameters.

e.g.

```
List<Employees> empList = new List<Employees>()
{
new Employees{ Id = 1, Name = "Name1", DeptName = "it",
Salary = 1000 },
new Employees{ Id = 2, Name = "Name2", DeptName = "acc",
Salary = 2000 },
new Employees{ Id = 3, Name = "Name3", DeptName = "dev",
Salary = 3000 },
new Employees{ Id = 4, Name = "Name4", DeptName = "qa",
Salary = 4000 }
};
Func<Employees, string> selector = x => x.Name + " Lamda";
IEnumerable<string> result = empList.Select(selector);
// output :
// Name1 Lamda
...
```

Func with more than 1 inout parameters :-

```
//func delegate with more than 1 input params
Func<List<Employees>, List<Department>, bool> multiFunc =
(emp, dept) =>
{
return emp.Any(e => dept.Any(d => d.DeptName ==
e.DeptName));
};
bool ifDept = multiFunc(empList, deptList);
```

Q34. WHAT IS ACTION DELEGATE ?

Action is also a delegate type defined in the **System namespace**.
1. An Action type delegate is the same as Func delegate except that the Action delegate **doesn't return a value**.
2. Action delegate can be used with a method that has a **void return type**.
3. It has 16 overloaded variation i.e it can take upto 16 input parameters.

Syntax : **Action<in T1, in T2,...>**

e.g.

```
Action<string> print = msg => Console.WriteLine(msg);
print("success");
```

Q35. WHAT IS PREDICATE DELEGATE ?

A predicate is also a delegate like Func and Action delegates.
1. It represents a method that contains a set of criteria and checks whether the passed parameter meets those criteria or not.
2. A predicate delegate methods **must take one input parameter**
3. It then **returns a boolean value** - true or false.
4. It has only 1 variation in which **only 1 parameter is passed**

Syntax : **Predicate<in T1>**

e.g.

```
Predicate<string> pred = x => x == "test";
pred("test");
//output :
//true
```

Q36. WHAT ARE ENUMS ?

- Enums are strongly typed constants
- Makes code more readable and maintainable
- Underlying Default type of enum is int
- Default value of first element is 0 and is incremented by 1

- Enums are value type
- Static GetValues() and GetNames() are used to get underlying type values and names

e.g.

```
using System;

public class Program
{
public static void Main()
{
//names of enum
string[] names = Enum.GetNames(typeof(Gender));
foreach(string name in names)
{
Console.WriteLine(name);
}
//values of enum
short[] shortValues = (short[])Enum.GetValues(typeof(Gender));
foreach(short shortValue in shortValues)
{
Console.WriteLine(shortValue);
}
}
}
public enum Gender : short
{
  Male = 1,
  Female,
  Unknown
}
/*Output :
Male
Female
Unknown
```

Q37. WHAT ARE TYPES AND TYPE MEMBERS ?

- **Types: -** Classes, Structs, Enums, delegates, interfaces are types
- **Type Members: -** Fields, Properties, constructors, methods are type members

(**Type members**) can have **ALL** access modifiers but (**Types**) can only have 2 access modifiers I.e. (**public and internal**)

Q38. WHAT ARE ACCESS MODIFIERS IN C# ?

The 5 access modifiers are: -
1. Private (***default for type members***)
2. Public
3. Protected
4. Internal (***default for Types***)
5. Protected internal

Note: any other access modifier with Types will result in compile time error.

Access modifier	Accessibility
Private (***default for type members***)	Only within containing class
Public	Anywhere
Protected	• Within containing type and types derived from containing type • To access base class members, we can either use **base** or **this** keywords e.g. base.ID or this.ID
Internal (***default for Types***)	Anywhere within containing assembly

Protected internal	Anywhere within containing assembly and from within a **derived class of any other assembly**

Q39. DIFFERENCE BETWEEN STRING AND STRINGBUILDER ?

string	StringBuilder
Immutable I.e., every time a string is manipulated a new reference is created	**Mutable** I.e., only one reference is created irrespective of string manipulations
Performance suffers as new references are created every time string is manipulated	**Better performance** in case of heavy string manipulations since creation of new references are muted
Namespace:- System	Namespace: - System.Text

Q40. WHAT IS VERBATIM LITERAL?

verbatim literal is a string, with an @ symbol prefix e.g .@"Some String"

Q41. WHAT ARE EXTENSION METHODS ?

- C# extension methods allows developers to **extend functionality of an existing type** without creating a new derived type, recompiling, or otherwise modifying the original type.
- An extension method is a **static method of a static class,**
- where the **"this"** modifier is applied to the **first parameter.**
- The **type of the first parameter will be the type that is extended.**

Q42. WHAT ARE BENEFITS OF EXTENSION METHODS ?

1. Extension methods allow existing classes to be extended without relying on inheritance or having to change the class's source code.
2. If the class is sealed than there in no concept of extending its functionality.For this a new concept is introduced, in other words extension methods.

Q43. EXPLAIN ANY PRACTICAL EXAMPLE OF EXTENSION METHODS ?

e.g.

```csharp
// program.cs
string str = "";
if (str.IN("Search1", "Search2"))
{
    // do smthing
}
```

```csharp
//Extensions.cs
using System;
using System.Linq;

namespace CSharp
{
 public static class Extensions
 {
    public static bool IN(this string sourceString, params string[]
argsList)
{
argsList.ToList().RemoveAll(x => string.IsNullOrEmpty(x));

if (!string.IsNullOrEmpty(sourceString) && argsList.Length > 0)
{
if (argsList.Any(x => x.Trim().Equals(sourceString.Trim(),
StringComparison.CurrentCultureIgnoreCase)))
```

```
return true;
else
return false;
}
return false;
}

public static bool AND(this string sourceString, params string[]
argsList)
{
argsList.ToList().RemoveAll(x => string.IsNullOrEmpty(x));

if (!string.IsNullOrEmpty(sourceString) && argsList.Length > 0)
{
if (argsList.All(x => x.Trim().Equals(sourceString.Trim(),
StringComparison.CurrentCultureIgnoreCase)))
return true;
else
return false;
}
return false;
}
}
}
```

Q44. DIFFERENCE BETWEEN LAZY VS EAGER LOADING ?

Eager loading	Lazy loading
All the data is retrieved in a single query	Only retrieve just the amount of data that we need in single query
We are trading memory consumption for database round	When we need more data, additional queries are issued to

trips	DB. Means more round trips to DB server. This round trips cause major performance bottleneck. Lesser the round trips, better the performance

Q45. WHEN TO USE EAGER AND LAZY LOADING ?

Eager loading :-

Load all needed entities at once i.e related objects (child objects) are loaded automatically with its parent object

Lazy loading :-

Related objects (child objects) are not loaded automatically with its parent object until they are requested.

By default LINQ supports lazy loading.

When to use : -

Eager loading	Lazy loading
When the relations are not too much	When using one-to-many collections
When you are sure that you will be using related entites with the main entity everywhere	When you are sure that you are not using related entitites instantly

Q46. LAZY VS EAGER INITIALIZATION IN SINGLETON ?

Lazy Loading : -

- Improves the performance
- Avoids unnecessary load till the point object is accessed
- Reduces the memory footprint on the start up
- Faster application load

Non-lazy or Eager loading :-

- Pre-instantiation of the object
- Commonly used in lower memory footprints

e.g.

E.g: - Lazy loading Singleton

```csharp
/// <summary>
/// 1. By default, Lazy<T> objects are thread-safe
/// </summary>
public sealed class LazySingleton
{
  static int instanceCounter = 0;
  private static readonly Lazy<LazySingleton>    singleInstance =
new Lazy<LazySingleton>(() => new             LazySingleton());


private LazySingleton()
 {
    instanceCounter++;
Console.WriteLine("Instances created"+instanceCounter);
 }


public static LazySingleton SingleInstance
 {
   get
   {
     return singleInstance.Value;
   }
 }
public  void LogMessage(string message)
 {
   Console.WriteLine("Message " + message);
 }
}
```

Q47. WHAT IS DIFFERENCE BETWEEN STATIC VS SINGLETON ?

1. **Singleton can be extended** :- Singleton classes support Interface inheritance whereas a static class cannot implement an interface
2. Since singleton class supports interface implementation, we can reuse our singleton for any number of implementations of interface confirming objects.
3. In case you need to have **more than 1 instance in future**,in Singleton class, you can make constructor public while is not possible with static classes
4. Unlike static classes, we can use singletons as parameters to methods, or objects.
5. The advantage of using a static class is that the compiler makes sure that no instance methods are accidentally added. The compiler guarantees that instances of the class cannot be created.

Q48. WHAT IS DIFFERENCE BETWEEN STACK VS HEAP ?

- All the **static** variables go to the **High Frequency Heap** in memory.
- Objects in **High Frequency Heap** is not garbage collected by GC and hence static variables available throughout life time of an application.
- We need to explicitly de-allocate it then we have to set it to **null** so that GC can clear it's allocated memory.

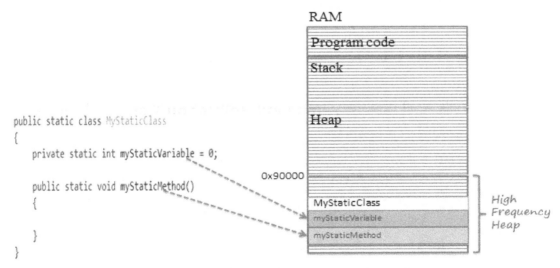

Memory allocation for Static fields

Stack	Heap
Value types like int,float etc.	Reference types like string, class objects etc.

Q49. WHAT IS SINGLETON DESIGN PATTERN ?

- **Creational type** of design pattern
- Ensures a class has only **one instance** and provides a global point of access to it
- Single thread-safe object is shared
- Example: - [log writer class]

ADVANTAGES OF SINGLETON

1. Singleton makes sure every client accesses it with **no Deadlock** or conflict.
2. It only allows **one instance** of a class responsible for sharing the resource, across the application.

GUIDELINES (PS3)

1. **PRIVATE CONSTRUCTOR**:-The singleton's class constructors should be private so that no external class can directly instantiate the Singleton class.
2. **SINGLE INSTANCE**:-It should create only one instance of the class
3. **STATIC PROPERTY/METHOD**:-There should be a static property/method that takes care of singleton class instantiation and that property should be shared across applications and is solely responsible for returning a singleton instance.
4. **SEALED CLASS**:-The C# singleton class should be sealed so that it could not be inherited by any other nested class.

Singleton real world usage :-
- Logging
- Managing database connections
- Configuration

Let's see how Singleton pattern is implemented:-

1. Thread safe Singleton :-

- Thread-safe.
- The biggest problem with this is performance; performance suffers since a lock is required every time an instance is requested.

```
Public sealed class SingletonBasic
{
Private static inti = 0;
Private SingletonBasic()
{
i++;
}

Private static readonly object padlock = newobject();
Private static SingletonBasic instance1 = null;
Public static SingletonBasic Instance
{
 get
 {
  lock (padlock)
  {
   if (instance1 == null)
   {
     instance1 = new SingletonBasic();
   }
    return instance1;
  }
 }
}

Public void Logwriter()
{
```

```
Console.WriteLine($"log{i}");
Console.ReadLine();
}
}
```

2. Thread Safety Singleton using Double Check Locking

```
Public class SingleTon
{
Private SingleTon()
{
Console.WriteLine("Singleton instance is created in CONSTRUCTOR.");
}
Private static object lockingObject = newobject();
Private static SingleTonsingleTonObject;
Public static SingleTonInstanceCreation()
{
if (singleTonObject == null)
{
lock (lockingObject)
{
if (singleTonObject == null)
{
   singleTonObject = newSingleTon();
}
}
}
Return singleTonObject;
}
}
```

3. Thread Safe Singleton without using locks

```
Public sealed class SingletonSession
{
```

```
Private SingletonSession()
{
Console.WriteLine($"Singleton instance is created in STATIC
CONSTRUCTOR.");
}


Private static SingletonSession _instance;

Public static SingletonSession Instance
{
get
{
return _instance ?? (_instance = new SingletonSession());
}
}


Public string UserName
{
get
{
Return
System.Security.Principal.WindowsIdentity.GetCurrent().Name;
}
}


}
```

4.Lazy Singleton:
- By default, Lazy<T> objects are **thread-safe**
- Lazy initialization is a technique that defers the creation of an object until the first time it is needed.
- In other words, **initialization** of the object happens only **on demand**.

Benefits:-
1. improves the **performance**

2. **avoid unnecessary load** till the point object is accessed
3. Reduces the memory footprint on the start-up
4. **faster** application load

Non-Lazy or eager loading:-

1. pre-instantiation of the object
2. commonly used in lower memory footprints

e.g.:-

```csharp
public sealed class LazySingleton
{
static int instanceCounter = 0;
private static readonly Lazy<LazySingleton>singleInstance = new
Lazy<LazySingleton>(() =>new LazySingleton());

private LazySingleton()
{
instanceCounter++;
Console.WriteLine("Instances created " + instanceCounter);
}

public static LazySingleton SingleInstance
{
get
{
return singleInstance.Value;
}
}

public void LogMessage(string message)
{
Console.WriteLine("Message " + message);
}
}
```

Q50. WHY WE NEED TO SEAL A SINGLETON CLASS?

Private constructor only prevents instantiation of objects from external class but **a nested child class can still inherit a Singleton class**. So, to avoid this inheritance from a nested child class we use sealed for singleton class.

```csharp
public class SealedSingleton
{
    private static SealedSingleton instance = null;
    private static int counter = 0;
    private SealedSingleton()
    {
        counter++;
        Console.WriteLine($"counter : {counter}");
        Console.ReadLine();
    }
    public static SealedSingleton Instance
    {
        get
        {
            if(instance==null)
            {
                instance = new SealedSingleton();
            }
            return instance;
        }
    }
    public void Print(string msg)
    {
        Console.WriteLine($"print : {msg}");
        Console.ReadLine();
```

```
        }
//Note : Nested class can still inherit Singleton class ,if it  is not sealed


    public class Child : SealedSingleton
    {
      public Child()
      {
      }
      public void childPrint(string msg)
      {
        Console.WriteLine($"Child print : {msg}");
        Console.ReadLine();
      }
    }
  }


[Main program]
  //Note : Singleton class constructor is called 1st time
  SealedSingleton obj = SealedSingleton.Instance;
  obj.Print("call 1");

  //Note : Singleton class constructor is called 2nd time
  Child childObj = new Child();
  childObj.childPrint("child call");
```

Note: Since, Singleton Constructor is called more than once, hence Singleton design pattern fails in this case.

Q51. WHAT IS A FACTORY DESIGN PATTERN ?

- **Creation design pattern**
- Define **an Interface** and let subclasses decide which class to instantiate

Advantage:-

- **Loose Coupling**: - Application will work with any class that implements Interface

Usage:-

- When client needs to specify class name to create objects

  e.g.

```
Interface IGet
{
stringConC(string s1, string s2);
}
Class clsFirst : IGet
{
public string ConC(string s1, string s2)
{
string Final = "From First: " + s1+" and " + s2;
return Final;
}
}
Class clsFactory
{
static public IGetCreateandReturnObj(int cChoice)
{
IGetObjSelector = null;
switch (cChoice)
{
case 1: ObjSelector = new clsFirst();
break;
case 2: ObjSelector = new clsSecond();
break;
default: ObjSelector = new clsFirst();
break;
}
returnObjSelector;
}
}
```

```
classclsSecond : IGet
{
public string ConC(string s1, string s2)
{
string Final = "From Second: " + s1 + " and " + s2;
return Final;
}
}
private void cmbSelect_SelectedIndexChanged(object sender,
EventArgs e)
{
IGetObjIntrface = null;
ObjIntrface =
clsFactory.CreateandReturnObj(cmbSelect.SelectedIndex + 1);
string res = ObjIntrface.ConC("First", "Second");
lblResult.Text = res;
}
```

Q52. WHAT IS A ADAPTER PATTERN ?

- **Structural design pattern**
- It acts as wrapper between two objects i.e. converts the interface of one class into another interface as per requirement
- Also known as **Wrapper**

Advantage:-

- Allows interaction of **incompatible** objects
- **Reusability** of existing functionality

Usage:-

- Using modern classes in Legacy code

e.g.

```csharp
public interface ITarget
{
string GetRequest();
}
//incomptaible interface with current code
public class Adaptee
{
public string GetSpecificRequest()
{
return"Specific request.";
}
}
//Adapter makes Adaptee's interface compatible with target's
interface
class Adapter : ITarget
{
private readonly Adaptee _adaptee;
public Adapter(Adaptee adaptee)
{
this._adaptee = adaptee;
}

public string GetRequest()
{
return $"This is '{this._adaptee.GetSpecificRequest()}'";
}
}

//Main.cs
public static void Main(string[] args)
{
Adaptee adaptee = new Adaptee();
ITarget target = new Adapter(adaptee);

Console.WriteLine("Adaptee interface is incompatible with the
```

```
client.");
Console.WriteLine("But with adapter client can call it's method.");

Console.WriteLine(target.GetRequest());
}
```

Q53. WHAT IS A OBSERVER PATTERN ?

- **Behavioral pattern**
- A **subscription** mechanism to notify dependent objects whenever state of one object changes
- One-to-many dependency between objects
- Also known as **publisher-subscribe**

Advantages:-

- Allows coupling between objects and observers
- Support for broadcast type communication

Usage:-

- When change in 1 object needs to be reflected in other object without tight coupling

Subject and observers:-

- Subject is an object which takes the responsibility to notify the observers of any changes e.g. database changes, property change etc.
- Observer is an object listening to subject changes

e.g.

```
//subject interface
internal interface ISubject
{
void Register(IObserver observer);
void UnRegister(IObserver observer);
void Notify();
```

```csharp
}
//observer interface
internal interface IObserver
{
void Update(double price);
}
//concrete subject
internal class ServiceSubject : ISubject
{
private double _price;

private List<IObserver>listObservers = new List<IObserver>();


public double price
{
get { return _price; }
set
{
if (_price != value)
{
_price = value;
Notify();
}
}
}

public void Notify()
{
listObservers.ForEach(x =>x.Update(price));
}

public void Register(IObserver observer)
{
listObservers.Add(observer);
```

```csharp
}

public void UnRegister(IObserver observer)
{
listObservers.Remove(observer);
}
}

//concrete observer
internal class ConcreteObserver : IObserver
{
private string _name;
public ConcreteObserver(string name)
{
this._name = name;
}

public void Update(double price)
{
Console.WriteLine($"Notified: updated price of stock {_name}is
{price}");
Console.ReadLine();
}
}

//Main class
public static void Main(string[] args)
{
ServiceSubject serviceSubject = new ServiceSubject();
// Add stocks
serviceSubject.Register(newConcreteObserver("IBM"));
serviceSubject.Register(newConcreteObserver("Google"));
serviceSubject.Register(newConcreteObserver("Reliance"));
//Stock prices update
serviceSubject.price = 100;
```

```
serviceSubject.price = 200;
}
```

Q54. WHAT ARE SOLID PRINCIPLES ?

The SOLID principles of Object Oriented Design include these five principles:
1. **SRP** – Single Responsibility Principle.
2. **OCP** – Open/Closed Principle.
3. **LSP** – Liskov Substitution Principle.
4. **ISP** – Interface Segregation Principle.
5. **DIP** – Dependency Inversion Principle.

1. SRP – Single Responsibility Principle

This means that every class, or similar structure, in your code should have only one job to do.
The Single Responsibility Principle is one of the SOLID design principles.We can define it in the following ways,

1. One reason to change
A class or method should have only one reason to change.

2. Single Responsibility
A class or method should have only a single responsibility.

SRP Benefits : -

The SRP has many benefits to improve code complexity and maintenance.Some benefits of SRP are following :

1. Reduction in complexity of a code
A code is based on its functionality.A method holds logic for a single functionality or task. So, it reduces the code complexity.

2.Increased readability, extensibility, and maintenance
As each method has a single functionality so it is easy to read and maintain.

3.Reusability and reduced error
As code separates based functionality so if the same functionality uses somewhere else in an application then don't write it again.

4.Better testability
In the maintenance, when a functionality changes then we don't need to test the entire model.

5.Reduced coupling
It reduced the dependency code.A method's code doesn't depend on other methods.

2.OCP – Open / Closed Principle

The principle says "A software module /class should be **open for extension**, but **closed for modification**".
 1. One should not modify an implementation(of a class or function) of logic and/or functionality.
 2. But the implementation(of a class or function) is open for extension,
  in other words one can extend the implementation(of a class or function) of logic and/or functionality.

3.LSP – Liskov Substitution Principle

The Liskov Substitution Principle(LSP) states that "you should be able to **use any derived class instead of a parent class** and have it behave in the same manner without modification".

 it means, when we have a base class and child class relationship, then, if we can successfully replace the object/instance of a parent class with an object/instance of the child class, without affecting the results that we get with the base class instance, then the two classes confirm to this principle.

4.ISP – Interface Segregation Principle.(Segregation = Separation, disconnection)

The Interface Segregation Principle states "that clients should not be forced to implement interfaces they don't use.
Instead of one fat interface many small interfaces are preferred based on groups of methods, each one serving one sub module.".

5.DIP – Dependency Inversion Principle

1.The Dependency Inversion Principle(DIP) states that **high - level modules /** classes should not depend on low -level modules / classes.Both **should depend upon abstractions.**

2. Secondly, abstractions should not depend upon details. **Details should depend upon abstractions.**

Q55. WHAT IS INVERSION OF CONTROL ?

Inversion of control is the actual mechanism using which we can make the higher level modules to depend on abstractions rather than concrete implementation of lower level modules.

GENERICS

Q56. WHAT ARE GENERICS ?

- Generic means the general form
- Not specific to a particular data type
- Generic classes and methods combine **reusability, type safety, and efficiency**

- One of the most significant features of Generics is **Type Safety**
- A generic type is declared by specifying a type parameter in an angle brackets after a type name, e.g. TypeName<T> where T is a type parameter.
- **System.Collections.Generic** namespace includes generic collection types

Q57. WHAT ARE GENERICS COLLECTIONS IN C# ?

- **List<T>** : Generic List<T> contains elements of specified type. It grows automatically as you add elements in it.
- **Dictionary<TKey,TValue>** : Dictionary<TKey,TValue> contains key-value pairs.
- **Hashset<T>:** Hashset<T> contains non-duplicate elements. It eliminates duplicate elements.

Q58. WHAT ARE NON- GENERICS COLLECTIONS IN C# ?

- **System.Collections** namespace contains the non-generic collection types
- **ArrayList** : ArrayList stores objects of any type like an array. However, there is no need to specify the size of the ArrayList like with an array as it grows automatically.
- **Hashtable** : Hashtable stores key and value pairs. It retrieves the values by comparing the hash value of the keys.

Q59. WHAT IS DIFFERENCE BETWEEN HASHTABLE AND DICTIONARY ?

HASHTABLE	DICTIONARY

System.collections namespace	System.collections.generics namespace
Non-generic collection : - stores key-value pairs of **any data types**.	Generic collection : -stores key-value pairs of **specific data types only**
Hashtable **returns null** if we try to find a **key which does not exist**.	Dictionary **throws an exception** if we try to find a **key which does not exist**
Data retrieval is **slower** than dictionary because of boxing-unboxing.	Data retrieval is **faster** than Hashtable.

Q60. WHAT IS DIFFERENCE BETWEEN ARRAY AND ARRAYLISTS ?

ARRAY	ARRAYLISTS
System namespace	**System.Collections** namespace
Array stores a **fixed number of elements**. The size of an Array must be specified at the time of initialization.	ArrayList **grows automatically** and you don't need to specify the size.

Array Declaration & Initialization:
int[] arr = new int[5]
int[] arr = new int[5]{1, 2, 3, 4, 5};
int[] arr = {1, 2, 3, 4, 5};
	ArrayList Declaration & Initialization:
	ArrayList arList = new ArrayList();
	arList.Add(1); // int
	arList.Add("One"); // string
	arList.Add(true); // bool

Array is **strongly typed**. This means that an array can store only specific type of items.	ArrayList can store **any type of items**.
Performs **faster** than ArrayList because it is strongly typed.	Performs **slows** because of boxing and unboxing.

Q61. WHAT IS DIFFERENCE BETWEEN IENUMERABLE AND LIST ?

IEnumerable	List
Read-only	Read-Write
To read, sort and/or filter your	To make permanent changes of any

collection, IEnumerable is sufficient	kind to your collection (add & remove), you'll need List
IEnumerable doesn't allow random access	List does allow random access using integral index

Q62. WHAT IS DIFFERENCE BETWEEN IENUMERABLE AND IQUERABLE ?

IEnumerable	IQuerable
System.Collections Namespace	**System.Linq** Namespace
doesn't support lazy loading	support lazy loading
Querying data from a database, IEnumerable execute a select query on the **server side**, **load data in-memory on a client-side and then filter data.**	Querying data from a database, IQueryable execute the select query on the **server side with all filters.**
When to use : When querying data from **in-memory collections** like List, Array, etc.	**When to use** : When querying data from **out-memory** (like remote database, service) collections.
Best Uses : In-memory traversal	Paging

Q63. WHAT IS DIFFERENCE BETWEEN BOXING AND UNBOXING ?

BOXING	UNBOXING
It convert **value** type into an reference/**object type**.	It convert an reference/**object** type into **value** type.
int val = 123;	int val = 123;

// Boxing
object o = val;
	// Boxing
	object o = val;
	// Unboxing
	int x = (int)o;

Value type is always stored in Stack	The Referenced Type is stored in Heap.

Q64. WHAT IS DIFFERENCE BETWEEN FOR AND FOREACH ?

FOR	FOREACH
There is need to specify the loop bounds (minimum or maximum)	You do not need to specify the loop bounds minimum or maximum
Using **for loop** we can iterate a collection in **both direction**, that is from index 0 to 9 and from 9 to 0.	using for-each loop, the iteration is possible in **forward direction only**.

e.g.
for (int i = 1; i <= 5; i++)
{
   i = i + i;
}
// This code will work as assignment is allowed here.
	foreach loop creates a copy of the collection on which you are iterating the loop. This means, if you want to perform an assignment operation on the collection item, you cannot directly perform on that item
	
	e.g.
	int[] tempArr = new int[] { 0, 1, 2, 3, 5, 8, 13 };
	foreach (int i in tempArr)
	{
	   i = i + 1;
	}
	//Error : - it's just a temporary variable and you cannot assign a value to it

Performance : - **faster** than foreach	Performance : - 'foreach' takes much

	time as compared to the 'for' loop because internally, it uses extra memory space, as well as, it uses GetEnumarator() and Next() methods of IEnumerables.
When to use: - when you want the performance, you should use a For loop instead	When to use:- when you want code to be readable and clean, you can use a Foreach loop

Q65. WHAT IS A YIELD KEYWORD ?

Yield keyword helps to do custom stateful iteration over a collection. Meaning when we use yield keyword the **control moves back and forth from the caller function to source and vice versa**.
yield keyword effectively creates a lazy enumeration over collection items that can be much more efficient.
e.g.

```
class Program {

static List<int> numbersList = new List<int> {

1, 2, 3, 4, 5

};

public static void Main() {

foreach(int i in YieldReturn()) {

Console.WriteLine(i);

}

Console.ReadLine();

}

public static IEnumerable<int> YieldReturn () {
```

```
int sum = 0;

foreach(int i in numbersList) {

sum += i;

yield return (sum);

}

}

}
```

Q66. WHAT IS DIFFERENCE BETWEEN SYNCHRONOUS AND ASYNCHRONOUS ?

Synchronization means two or more operations happen sequntially. Asnchonous means two or more operations are running in different contexts (thread) so that they can run concurrently and do not block each other. Asynchronous means two or more operations happen asynchronously.
if any process is blocked in a synchronous application, the whole application gets blocked, and our application stops responding until the whole task completes. Asynchronous programming is very helpful in this condition. By using Asynchronous programming, the Application can continue with the other work that does not depend on the completion of the entire task.

Q67. WHAT IS DEPENDENCY INVERSION PRINCIPLE ?

- High-level modules should not depend on low-level modules. Both should depend on abstractions
- Abstractions should not depend on details. Details should depend on abstractions.

- The interaction between high level and low level modules should be thought of as an Abstract interaction between them.

Presentation layer ⟶ **Business layer** ⟶ **DataAccess layer**

(Lower level) **(Higher level)**

For e.g :

Button click ⟶ **Save() method** ⟶ **Save data in DB**

Lower level modules are consumed by higher level modules which enable complexity. Higher level modules depends on lower level to achieve some task.

It limits reusability of higher level modules

Q68. WHAT IS INVERSION OF CONTROL (IOC) ?

- The inversion of control design pattern states that objects should not create objects on which they depend to perform some activity. Instead, they should get those objects from an outside service or a container.
- Inversion of control (IoC) is a design pattern in which the control flow of a program is inverted.
- You can take advantage of the inversion of control pattern to **decouple the components** of your application and make your application modular and testable.
- IOC allows achieving **loose coupling** between different objects.
- IOC can be applied using interface or abstaction class
- If we want to make one class independent from other class then you have to apply abstraction (interface) which mediates the Interaction between classes.
- Dependency injection is a subset of the inversion of control principle. In other words, dependency injection is just one way of implementing inversion

of control. You can also implement inversion of control using delegates, factory method etc.

Q69. WHAT IS DEPENDENCY INJECTION (DI) ?

Dependency Injection (DI) is a design pattern used to implement IoC. It allows the creation of dependent objects outside of a class and provides those objects to a class through different ways. Using DI, we move the creation and binding of the dependent objects outside of the class that depends on them.

The Dependency Injection pattern involves 3 types of classes.

1. **Client Class:** The client class (dependent class) is a class which depends on the service class
2. **Service Class:** The service class (dependency) is a class that provides service to the client class.
3. **Injector Class:** The injector class injects the service class object into the client class.

The injector class creates an object of the service class, and injects that object to a client object. In this way, the DI pattern separates the responsibility of creating an object of the service class out of the client class.

Q70. WHAT ARE TYPES OF DEPENDENCY INJECTION (DI) ?

The injector class injects the service (dependency) to the client (dependent). The injector class injects dependencies broadly in three ways: through a constructor, through a property, or through a method.

Constructor Injection: In the constructor injection, the injector supplies the service (dependency) through the client class constructor.

Property Injection: In the property injection (aka the Setter Injection), the injector supplies the dependency through a public property of the client class.

Method Injection: In this type of injection, the client class implements an interface which declares the method(s) to supply the dependency and the injector uses this interface to supply the dependency to the client class.

e.g. **Constructor Injection**

```csharp
//Created IAccount interface to make code loosely coupled.
public interface IAccount
{
   void PrintData();
}
//Implemented the IAccount interface in SavingAccount class
public class SavingAccount : IAccount
{
   public void PrintData()
   {
     Console.WriteLine("Saving account data.");
   }
}
//Implemented the IAccount interface in CurrentAccount class
public class CurrentAccount : IAccount
{
   public void PrintData()
   {
     Console.WriteLine("Current account data.");
   }
}
//Account class(high level module) is not depended on any other classes.
//So now it is loosely coupled.
public class Account
{
    private IAccount account;
```

```csharp
        //Passing IAccount interface as parameter to Account constructor
        // Constructor Injection
        public Account(IAccount account)
        {
            this.account = account;
        }
        public void PrintAccounts()
        {
            account.PrintData();
        }
    }
class Program
{
    static void Main()
    {
// Passing savingAccount object in Account class
        IAccount savingAccount = new SavingAccount();
        Account account = new Account(savingAccount);
        account.PrintAccounts();
    // Passing currentAccount object in Account class
        IAccount currentAccount = new CurrentAccount();
        account = new Account(currentAccount);
        account.PrintAccounts();
        Console.ReadLine();
    }
}
```

e.g. **Property Injection**

```csharp
//Created IAccount interface to make code loosely coupled.
public interface IAccount
{
    void PrintData();
}
```

```csharp
//Implemented the IAccount interface in SavingAccount class
public class SavingAccount : IAccount
{
    public void PrintData()
    {
        Console.WriteLine("Saving account data.");
    }
}
    //Implemented the IAccount interface in SavingAccount class
public class CurrentAccount : IAccount
{
    public void PrintData()
    {
        Console.WriteLine("Current account data.");
    }
}


//Account class is not depended on any other classes.
//So now it is loosely coupled.
public class Account
{
// Property injection
//Here my account property is of type IAccount interface
    public IAccount account { get; set; }

    public void PrintAccounts()
    {
        account.PrintData();
    }
}
 class Program
{
    static void Main()
    {
```

```csharp
//calling savingAccount object using property
Account savingAccount = new Account();
savingAccount.account = new SavingAccount();
savingAccount.PrintAccounts();
//calling currentAccount object using property
Account currentAccount = new Account();
currentAccount.account = new CurrentAccount();
currentAccount.PrintAccounts();
  Console.ReadLine();
 }
}
```

e.g. **Method Injection**

```csharp
//Created IAccount interface to make code loosely coupled.
public interface IAccount
{

  void PrintData();
}
 //Implemented the IAccount interface in SavingAccount class
public class SavingAccount : IAccount
{

  public void PrintData()
  {

    Console.WriteLine("Saving account data.");
  }
}
 //Implemented the IAccount interface in SavingAccount class
public class CurrentAccount : IAccount
{

  public void PrintData()
  {

    Console.WriteLine("Current account data.");
  }
}
```

```csharp
//Account class is not depended on any other classes.
//So now it is loosely coupled.
public class Account
{
  // Method injection
  //Passing "IAccount" as parameter to PrintAccounts() method
  public void PrintAccounts(IAccount account)
  {
    account.PrintData();
  }
}
 class Program
{
  static void Main()
  {
    //calling savingAccount object using method
    Account savingAccount = new Account();
    savingAccount.PrintAccounts(new SavingAccount());
    //calling currentAccount object using method
    Account currentAccount = new Account();
    currentAccount.PrintAccounts(new CurrentAccount());
          Console.ReadLine();
  }
}
```

Q71. WHAT ARE BENEFITS OF DEPENDENCY INJECTION (DI) ?

What we gain by following dependency injection is **loosely coupled code**. And loosely coupled code is key in achieving some desirable properties in your code:

- **Extensibility** – makes is possible to add new functionality by simply providing a different implementation of the interface and provides a natural hook for patterns like decorators, adapters, composites, facades, etc

- **Testability** - Code can be independently tested, and test mocks injected during tests.
- **Maintainability** - Having code which is both extensible and testable goes at great lengths towards enabling maintainability!

Dependency Injection is also a key tool that helps you adhere to the **SOLID** principles

- **Open-Closed principle.** The interfaces and declaration of dependencies provide a natural hook to add new functionality to the system without modifying the existing code.
- **Dependency Inversion.** Your higher-level modules (the ones implementing your important core business logic) can declare and control the interfaces they need, for lower level modules to implement.

MEMORY MANAGEMENT

Q72. WHAT IS GARBAGE COLLECTOR (GC) ?

- The Garbage Collector (GC) is the part of the .NET Framework that allocates and releases memory for your .NET applications.
- The process of releasing memory is called garbage collection. It releases only objects that are no longer being used in the application
- The .NET objects are allocated to a region of memory termed the managed heap. They will be automatically destroyed by the garbage collector.
- Heap allocation only occurs when you are creating instances of classes.
- Objects are allocated in the heap continuously, one after another
- This reuse of memory helps reduce the amount of total memory that a program needs to run.

Q73. How GC differentiate between reachable and unreachable objects ?

- A **root** is a storage location containing a reference to an object on the managed heap.
- The runtime will check objects on the managed heap to determine whether they are still **reachable** (in other words, **rooted**) by the application.
- The CLR builds an **object graph**, that represents each **reachable object** on the heap. Object graphs are used to document all reachable objects.
e.g.

Assume the managed heap contains a set of objects named A, B, C, D, E, F and G. During a garbage collection, these objects are examined for active roots. After the graph has been constructed, unreachable objects are marked as garbage in reddish color.

- After the objects have been marked for termination, they are deleted from memory. At this point, the remaining space on the heap is compacted, that in turn causes the CLR to modify the set of active application roots to refer to the correct memory location.
- The next object pointer is readjusted to point to the next available slot.

Q74. What are conditions in which GC will be called ?

Garbage collection occurs when one of the following conditions is true:

- The system has **low physical memory**. This is detected by either the low memory notification from the OS or low memory as indicated by the host.
- The memory that's used by allocated objects on the managed heap **surpasses an acceptable threshold**. This threshold is continuously adjusted as the process runs.

- The **GC.Collect method is called**. In almost all cases, you don't have to call this method, because the garbage collector runs continuously. This method is primarily used for unique situations and testing.

Q75. WHAT ARE GC GENERATIONS ?

- For better performance of memory releasing, the managed heap is divided into segments called "Generations".
- There are only **3 generations: 0, 1 and 2.**
- Longer an object has existed on the heap are reachable objects. Objects that have only recently been placed on the heap are unreachable.
- During a full garbage collection, the GC must pass through all objects in the heap, so this process might have a great impact on system resources.

1. When objects are just created, they are placed to the **Generation 0** (Gen 0).
2. When Gen 0 is full, the GC performs a garbage collection. During the collection, the GC removes all unreachable objects from the heap. All reachable objects are promoted to the **Generation 1** (Gen 1). The Gen 0 collection is a rather quick operation.
3. When Gen 1 is full, the Gen 1 garbage collection is performed. All objects that survive the collection are promoted to **Gen 2**. The Gen 0 collection also takes place here.
4. When Gen 2 is full, the GC performs full garbage collection. First, Gen 2 collection is performed, then the Gen 1 and Gen 0 collections take place. If there is still not enough memory for new allocations, the GC raises the **OutOfMemory exception**.

Q76. HOW UNMANAGED RESOURCES ARE CLEANED UP ?

- For most of the objects that your application creates, you can rely on garbage collection to automatically perform the necessary memory management tasks. However, **unmanaged resources require explicit cleanup**.
- The most common type of unmanaged resource is an object that wraps an operating system resource, such as a file handle, window handle, or network connection
- Garbage collector doesn't have specific knowledge about how to clean up the resource.
- By providing a **Dispose** method, you enable users of your object to explicitly free its memory when they are finished with the object.

Q77. WHAT IS DISPOSE ?

- Performs application-defined tasks associated with freeing, releasing, or resetting **unmanaged resources.**
- There are a couple of resources which GC is not able to release as it doesn't have information that, how to claim memory from those resources like File handlers, window handlers, network sockets, database connections etc. If your application these resources than it's programs responsibility to release unmanaged resources.
- If you are using a class that implements the **IDisposable interface**, you should call its **Dispose implementation** when you are finished using the class.

Q78. WHAT IS FINALIZE ?

- **Finalize method also called destructor** to the class.
- Finalize method **can not be called explicitly** in the code.

- Only Garbage collector can call the the Finalize when object become inaccessible. Finalize method cannot be implemented directly it can only be implement via declaring destructor.
- After compilation destructor becomes Finalize method.

e.g.

```
public class MyClass: IDisposable {

  public MyClass() {

    //Initialization:

  }

    //Destrucor also called Finalize

    ~MyClass() {

      this.Dispose();

    }

    public void Dispose() {

      //write code to release unmanaged resource.

    }

}
```

Q79. WHEN FINALIZE SHOULD BE USED ?

There may be any *unmanaged resource* for example file stream declared at class level. We may not be knowing what stage or which step should be appropriate to close the file. This object is being use at many places in the application. So in this scenario Finalize can be appropriate location where unmanaged resource can be released. It means, clean the memory acquired by the unmanaged resource as soon as object is inaccessible to application.

Q80. WHICH IS MORE PREFERRABLE FINALIZE OR DISPOSE ?

- It is always recommended that, one should not implement the Finalize method until it is extremely necessary. First priority should always be to implement the Dispose method and clean unmanaged as soon as possible when processing finish with that.
- *Finalize is bit expensive to use*. It doesn't clean the memory immediately. Due to finalize method GC will not clear entire memory associated with object in first attempt.

Q81. WHAT IS PURPOSE OF USING STATEMENT ?

- Provides a convenient syntax that ensures the correct use of **IDisposable** objects.
- The C# using statement defines a boundary for the object outside of which, the object is automatically destroyed
- The objects specified within the using block must implement the IDisposable interface

e.g.

....

```
using (MyManagedClass mnObj = new MyManagedClass())
{
......
mnObj.Use(); //use the mnObj object
......
} //The compiler will dispose the mnObj object now
......
```

- The using statement ensures that Dispose (or DisposeAsync) is called even if an exception occurs within the using block.

- You can achieve the same result by putting the object inside a try block and then calling <u>Dispose</u> (or <u>DisposeAsync</u>) in a **finally** block; in fact, this is how the **using statement is translated by the compiler**.

e.g.

```
string textLines=@"text lines here";
{
  var reader = new StringReader(textLines);
  try {
    string? item;
    do {
      item = reader.ReadLine();
      Console.WriteLine(item);
    } while(item != null);
  } finally
  {
    reader?.Dispose();
  }
}
```

- Multiple instances of a type can be declared in a single using statement.

e.g.

```
string text1=@"text content 1";
string text2=@"text content 2";

using (StringReader left = new StringReader(text1),
  right = new StringReader(text2))
{
  string? item;
  do {
    item = left.ReadLine();
    Console.Write(item);
    Console.Write("   ");
    item = right.ReadLine();
    Console.WriteLine(item);
  } while(item != null);
}
```

LINQ

Q82. WHAT IS DIFFERENCE BETWEEN EAGER AND LAZY LOADING IN LINQ ?

Eager loading	Lazy Loading
All the data is retrieved in a **single query**, which can then be cached to improve the Application performance.	We only **retrieve** just the amount of **data, which we need in a single query**. When we need more data related to the initial data, additional queries are issued to the database
Performance - With Eager Loading, we are trading **memory consumption** for the database round trips	**Performance** - There are **several round trips** between the Application Server and the database Server. Lesser the round trips, better will be the performance
Usage - if you are displaying both Department and Employees data, then Eager Loading works best, as it avoids the additional round trips to the database.	**Usage -** if on a given page, you are only displaying Departments, then there is no reason for Eager Loading related Employees data. Hence, in this case, Lazy Loading works best.

Note* : If you are not sure of what data is exactly needed, start with Lazy Loading and if it is leading to N + 1 problem then Eager Loading handles the data better.

Q83. WHAT IS LAZY/DEFFERED LOADING IN LINQ ?

In case of lazy loading, related objects (child objects) are not loaded automatically with its parent object until they are requested. **By default LINQ supports lazy loading.**

e.g.

```
var query = context.Categories.Take(3); // Lazy loading
foreach (var Category in query)
{
Console.WriteLine(Category.Name);
 foreach (var Product in Category.Products)
```

```
{
Console.WriteLine(Product.ProductID);
}
}
```

In above example, you have 4 SQL queries which means calling the database 4 times, one for the Categories and three times for the Products associated to the Categories. In this way, child entity is populated when it is requested.

Turn off Lazy Loading : -
You can turn off the lazy loading feature by setting **LazyLoadingEnabled** property of the ContextOptions on context to false. Now you can fetch the related objects with the parent object in one query itself.
e.g.
```
context.ContextOptions.LazyLoadingEnabled = false;
```

Q84. WHAT IS EAGER LOADING IN LINQ ?

In case of eager loading, related objects (child objects) are loaded automatically with its parent object. To use Eager loading you need to use **Include()** method.

e.g.

```
var query = context.Categories.Include("Products").Take(3); // Eager loading

 foreach (var Category in query)

{

Console.WriteLine(Category.Name);

 foreach (var Product in Category.Products)

{

Console.WriteLine(Product.ProductID);

}
```

}

In above example, you have only one SQL queries which means **calling the database only one time**, for the Categories and the Products associated to the Categories. In this way, child entity is populated with parent entity.

Q85. WHAT IS UNION IN LINQ ?

- Union combines multiple collections into a single collection and returns a resultant collection with unique elements
- **union two list without duplicates**

e.g.

```
int[] numbers = { 1, 2, 3, 4, 5 };
int[] numbers1 = { 4, 5, 6, 6, 7, 8, 9, 10 };
//union two list without duplicates
var unionList = numbers.Union(numbers1);
foreach (var item in unionList)
{
Console.WriteLine(item);
}
Console.ReadLine();
```

//Output : 1, 2, 3, 4, 5,6, 7, 8, 9, 10

Q86. WHAT IS INTERSECT IN LINQ ?

- Intersect returns sequence elements which are common in both the input Sequences
- **return common items from 2 lists**

e.g.

```
int[] numbers = { 1, 2, 3, 4, 5 };
int[] numbers1 = { 4, 5, 6, 6, 7, 8, 9, 10 };
```

```
//return common items from 2 lists
var intersectList = numbers.Intersect(numbers1);
foreach (var item in intersectList)
{
Console.WriteLine(item);
}
Console.ReadLine();
```

//Output : 4,5

Q87. WHAT IS EXCEPT IN LINQ ?

- Except returns sequence elements from the first input sequence that are not present in the second input sequence
- **Return elements from list1 that are not present in 2nd list**

e.g.

```
int[] numbers = { 1, 2, 3, 4, 5 };

int[] numbers1 = { 4, 5, 6, 6, 7, 8, 9, 10 };

//return elemets from list1 that r not present in 2nd list

var exceptList = numbers.Except(numbers1);

foreach (var item in exceptList)

{

Console.WriteLine(item);

}

Console.ReadLine();
```

//Output : 1,2,3

Q88. DIFFERENCE BETWEEN FIRST/FIRSTORDEFAULT AND SINGLE/SINGLEORDEFAULT ?

First() / FirstOrDefault()	Single() / SingleOrDefault()
First() returns the first element of a sequence even there is a single element in that sequence	Single() returns the single element of a sequence and that element should be the exactly a single one. If there are more then one matching elements the exception is thrown
First() simply **gives you the first one**.	Single() asserts that **one and only one element exists in the sequence**.
FirstOrDefault() - Same as First(), but not thrown any exception or return null when there is no result.	**SingleOrDefault()** – Same as Single(), but it can handle the null value. **SingleOrDefault()** will still throw an exception if Sequence contains more than one matching element
When to use Developer may use First () / FirstOrDefault() anywhere, when they required single value from collection or database.	**When to use** Use Single / SingleOrDefault() when you sure there is only one record present in database or you can say if you querying on database with help of primary key of table.

Note* : In the case of Fist / FirstOrDefault, only one row is retrieved from the database so it performs slightly better than single / SingleOrDefault.

Q89. SCENARIOS OF FIRST/FIRSTORDEFAULT AND SINGLE/SINGLEORDEFAULT ?

//first and single
List<int> lstCount = new List<int> { 10, 20, 30, 40, 50, 60, 70, 80, 90 };

var result1 = lstCount.**First**(x => x > 10);
Console.WriteLine("First : " + result1); **//20**

```
var result2 = lstCount.FirstOrDefault(x => x < 10);
Console.WriteLine("FirstOrDefault : " + result2); // 0


var result3 = lstCount.Single(x => x < 20);
Console.WriteLine("Single: " + result3); // 10


var result4 = lstCount.SingleOrDefault(x => x < 10);
Console.WriteLine("SingleOrDefault : " + result4);// 0


var result5 = lstCount.Single(x => x < 10);
Console.WriteLine("Single : " + result5);
//Error : Sequence contains no matching element'


var result6 = lstCount.SingleOrDefault(x => x > 10);
Console.WriteLine("SingleOrDefault : " + result6);
// Error : 'Sequence contains more than one matching element'


var result7 = lstCount.Single(x => x > 10);
Console.WriteLine("Single : " + result7);
// Error : 'Sequence contains more than one matching element'
Console.ReadLine();
```

Q90. WHAT IS ANY AND ALL IN LINQ ?

<u>Any</u> :

Returns **true if *at least one of the elements*** in the source sequence matches the provided **predicate**. Otherwise it returns false.

<u>All :</u>
Returns **true if *every element*** in the source sequence matches the provided **predicate**. Otherwise it returns false.

e.g.

```
//any or all
string[] names = { "abc", "zxc", "fgh" };
string[] namesAll = { "abc", "abc", "abc" };


var a = names.Any(x => x == "zxc"); // true
var b = namesAll.All(x => x == "abc"); // true
var c = names.All(x => x == "abc");// false
```

Q91. DIFFERENCE BETWEEN SELECT AND SELECTMANY ?

Select operator selects values from a collection whereas SelectMany Operator selects values from multiple collection or nested collection. SelectMany Operator selects values from multiple or nested collection and flatten the result.

e.g.

```
List<Employee> employees = new List<Employee>();
```

```
Employee emp1 = new Employee { Name = "Mark", Skills = new List<string> { "C", "C++", "Java" } };
```

```
Employee emp2 = new Employee { Name = "Ben", Skills = new List<string> { "SQL Server", "C#", "ASP.NET" } };
```

```
Employee emp3 = new Employee { Name = "Steve", Skills = new List<string> { "C#", "ASP.NET MVC", "Windows Azure", "SQL Server" } };
```

```
employees.Add(emp1);
```

```
employees.Add(emp2);
```

```
employees.Add(emp3);
```


```
// Query using Select()
```

```
IEnumerable<List<String>> resultSelect = employees.Select(e => e.Skills);
```

```
Console.WriteLine("*Select *");
```

```csharp
// Two foreach loops are required to iterate through the results
// because the query returns a collection of arrays.
foreach (List<String> skillList in resultSelect)
{
foreach (string skill in skillList)
{
Console.WriteLine(skill);
}
Console.WriteLine();
}
// Query using SelectMany()
IEnumerable<string> resultSelectMany = employees.SelectMany(emp =>
emp.Skills);
Console.WriteLine("* SelectMany *");
// Only one foreach loop is required to iterate through the results
// since query returns a one-dimensional collection.
foreach (string skill in resultSelectMany)
{
Console.WriteLine(skill);
}
```

Q92. HOW TO FLATTEN LIST OF LISTS USING LINQ ?

Using **selectMany** we can flatten list of lists

Q93. WHAT IS LINQ ?

LINQ stands for language integrated query. LINQ enables us to query any Type of data store (SQL server, XML documents, Objects in memory etc.)

Q94. WHY USE LINQ ?

- Linq enables us to work with different data sources with same code.
- Provides inteliisense
- Compile time error checking

Q95. WHAT ARE LINQ PROVIDERS ?

- LINQ provider is a component between the LINQ query and the actual data source
- It converts the LINQ query into the format that the corresponding data source can understand
- e.g., LINQ to SQL provider converts LINQ query to T-SQL that sql server database can understand.

Q96. WHAT ARE TYPES OF LINQ PROVIDERS ?

Some of the LINQ providers are: -
- LINQ to XML (XML Docs)
- LINQ to SQL (Databases)
- LINQ to Objects (Object Data)
- LINQ to Entities (Entities)
- LINQ to DataSet (Datasets)

e.g., LINQ on database
EmployeeDataContext dataContext = new EmployeeDataContext();
Var Datasource = from emp in dataContext.Students
Where emp.Gender == "Male"
Select emp;

e.g., LINQ on objects (in-memory objects like array, lists etc.)
Int[] numbers = {1,2,3,4,5,6,7,8,9,10}
Var Datasource = from number in numbers
where (number % 2) == 0
select number;

Q97. WHAT IS LAMBDA EXPRESSION ?

- Typically, lambda expression is a more *concise syntax of anonymous method*. It is just a new way to write anonymous method.
- At compile time all the lambda expressions are converted into anonymous methods
- The left side of the lambda operator "=>" represents the arguments of anonymous method and the right side represents the method body.

Lambda expression Syntax

(Input-parameters) => expression-or-statement-block

Types of Lambda expression

1. **Statement Lambda** - Statement lambda has a statement block on the right side of the lambda operator "=>".

x => { return x * x; };

2. **Expression Lambda** - Expression lambda has only an expression (no return statement or curly braces), on the right side of the lambda operator "=>".

x => x * x;

Q98. WHAT IS ANONYMOUS METHOD ?

- An anonymous method is an inline unnamed method in the code
- It is created using the delegate keyword and doesn't have its name and return type.
- An anonymous method has no name, optional parameters and return type; it has only body.

e.g.

```
class Program
{
//delegate for representing anonymous method
delegate int delPrint(int x, int y);
static void Main(string[] args)
{
//anonymous method using delegate keyword
delPrint d1 = delegate(int x, int y) { return x * y; };
int result = delPrint (4, 2);
Console.WriteLine(result);
}
}
//output:
8
```

Q99. WHAT IS GROUPBY IN LINQ ?

- The Linq GroupBy belongs to the Grouping Operators category
- This method takes a flat sequence of elements and then organizes the elements into groups (i.e. **IGrouping<TKey, TSource>**) based on a given key.

- It **return an IEnumerable<IGrouping<TKey, TSource>>** where TKey is nothing but the Key value on which the grouping has been formed and TSource is the collection of elements that matches the grouping key value.

e.g.

```
var result = listEmployess.GroupBy(x => x.Department);
```

e.g.: GroupBy with OrderBy

```
var resultGroup = listStudents.GroupBy(x => x.Branch).OrderBy(x => x.Key)
.Select(x => new
{
key = x.Key,
studentsOrder = x.OrderBy(y => y.Name)
});
foreach (var group in resultGroup)
{
//key name(Branch) - count
Console.WriteLine(group.key + "-" + group.studentsOrder.Count());
//iterate through each grouping
foreach (var item in group.studentsOrder)
{
Console.WriteLine(item.Name + " - " + item.Branch + " - " + item.Gender);
}
}
Console.Read();
```

Q100. HOW TO USE MULTIPLE KEYS GROUPBY IN LINQ ?

We may need to group the data based on multiple keys. In this case data returned is an anonymous type.

e.g.

```
var resultGroup = listStudents.GroupBy(x => new { x.Branch, x.Gender })
.OrderBy(x => x.Key.Branch).ThenBy(x => x.Key.Gender)
.Select(x=> new {
branch = x.Key.Branch,
gender = x.Key.Gender,
studentsOrder = x.OrderBy(y=>y.Name)
});
foreach (var group in resultGroup)
{
//key name(Branch,gender) - count
Console.WriteLine(group.branch + "-" + group.gender + "-" +
group.studentsOrder.Count());
//iterate through each grouping
foreach (var item in group.studentsOrder)
{
Console.WriteLine(item.Name + " - " + item.Branch + " - " + item.Gender);
}
}
Console.Read();
```

Q101. WHAT IS DIFFERENCE BETWEEN STRING.JOIN AND STRING.CONCAT ?

String.concat() - we must explicitly add the separator between each string
String.join() - Allows us to specify the separator as the first parameter.
In String.join atleast 2 paramerets are mandatory. First parameter should always be a separator of char or string type while second parameter should be a string which needs to be concatenated.
Performance: **string.join** consistently performs better.
e.g. : We are concatenating two strings with empty space as a separator.
string result = string.**concat**("The"," ","Test"); // We have explicitly added " " between 2 strings
//output : The Test
string resultJoin = string.**join**(' ',"The","Test");
//1st parameter will automatically add specified separator between all concatenated strings.
//output : The Test

Q102. WHAT IS DIFFERENCE BETWEEN STRING AND STRINGBUILDER ?

String
String is **immutable**, Immutable means if you create string object then you cannot modify it and It **always create new object** of string type in memory.
e.g.
string str = "This";
 // create a new string instance instead of changing the old one
 str += "is";
 str += "string test";

Stringbuilder
StringBuilder is **mutable**, means if create string builder object then you can perform any operation like insert, replace or append **without creating new instance** for every time.it will update string at one place in memory doesnt create new space in memory.
e.g.

```
StringBuilder sb = new StringBuilder("");
// do not create any new instances, will only update the already created instance
sb.Append("This");
sb.Append("is");
sb.Append("stringBuilder test ");
string strResult = sb.ToString();
```

Q103. WHAT IS DIFFERENCE BETWEEN READONLY AND CONST ?

Readonly	Const
ReadOnly is a runtime constant	Const is a compile time constant
The value of readonly field can be changed in constructor	The value of the const field can not be changed
It can be static	It cannot be static

Q104. WHAT IS DIFFERENCE BETWEEN VAR AND DYNAMIC ?

Var	Dynamic
Compile time – This means the type of variable declared is decided by the compiler at compile time.	**Run time** - This means the type of variable declared is decided by the compiler at runtime time.

Need to initialize at the time of declaration.
 	
e.g., var str="test string";
 	
Looking at the value assigned to the variable str, the compiler will treat the variable str as string.
	No need to initialize at the time of declaration.
	
	e.g., dynamic str;
	
	str="test string"; //Works fine and compiles
	
	str=2; //Works fine and compiles

Errors are caught at compile time	**Errors are caught at runtime**
Visual Studio shows intellisense	**Intellisense is not availabl**
e.g., var obj; will **throw a compile error** since the variable	e.g., dynamic obj; will **compile;**

is not initialized. The compiler needs that this variable should be initialized so that it can infer a type from the value.	
e.g var obj=1; obj="test string"; **will throw error** since the compiler has already decided that the type of obj is System.Int32 when the value 1 was assigned to it. Now assigning a string value to it violates the type safety.	e.g. dynamic obj=1; obj1="test string"; **will compile and run** since the compiler creates the type for obj as System.Int32 and then recreates the type as string This code will work fine.

About the Author

Vishal garg

Vishal Garg is a technical writer with a passion for writing technical books. He has passion for learning new technologies and share the knowledge with everyone. He is well versed in technologies like Azure, Devops, Angular, .Net core, C# etc. He also shares his knowledge with the community through book writings, blog writings , presentations etc.

He has written books on different technologies as well and got a positive reviews on that. He followed a very unique way to cover all major concepts.

With the help of various surveys and real time experience a question bank of a particular topic are compiled and logged in a book.

He is hoping that all readers will be benefited from this book and looking forward to put in more effort to produce quality books in future.

Note : If you like the book, please take some time to put in positive reviews on Amzon website. This feedback will encourage him to produce more quality books in future.

More Books by this Author

- .Net Core Simplified: Interview QA
- Angular Simplified: Learning made easy
- C# Interview Question and Answers: Simplified
- Azure Devops: Interview Questions and Answers